How to Overcome Fear

H.E. Metropolitan Youssef

ST. MARY & MOSES ABBEY PRESS

How to Overcome Fear

By Metropolitan Youssef

Designed & Published by:
St. Mary & St. Moses Abbey Press
101 S Vista Dr, Sandia, TX 78383
stmabbeypress.com

CONTENTS

Introduction

All of us, without exception, experience situations wherein we feel fear. Many of us, and perhaps most of us, have a fear of the unknown; for example, when a person immigrates to another country, not knowing what he will encounter there, he has a fear of the unknown future. Many of us have a fear of death, because our knowledge of what is after death is limited. Fear of the unknown is normal.

Some might have a fear of the future, because they do not know what will happen to them. This kind of fear causes many to become worried and troubled, especially young people who have completed their studies, yet fear that no suitable work opportunities will be available to them. Although things may go well for some presently, they still fear, as they are not sure that things will continue as such in the future.

There are young people who have a fear of loneliness, unable to manage the affairs of their lives. They may abandon the thought of marriage, in fear of being joined in marriage to the wrong person.

Others may have a fear of what might happen to them at work or in the current economy and what may arise from it (e.g., economic depression, unemployment and loss of their investments in banks or markets, as had happened in the global economic crisis that ravaged the world).

Some also may have a fear of failure at the work they have joined, or of passing exams lest they fail in them.

Also, many fathers and mothers get worried and fear for the future of their children, having many questions, for example: Will they be able to raise their children in the fear of God, or will they go astray when they grow up? Will they suffer from diseases, and will they succeed or fail in life?

Moreover, all people have a fear of sickness.

There is a story that came in the Book of Numbers (13:17–33), when Moses the prophet, according to God's command, sent twelve men, one from each tribe, to spy out the land of Canaan. The Holy Scripture says:

> Then Moses sent them to spy out the land of Canaan, and said to them, "Go up this way into the South, and go up to the mountains, and see what the land is like: whether the people who dwell in it are strong or weak, few or many; whether the land they dwell in is good or bad;

whether the cities they inhabit are like camps or strongholds; whether the land is rich or poor; and whether there are forests there or not. Be of good courage. And bring some of the fruit of the land." Now the time was the season of the first ripe grapes.[1]

He sent them so that they may present to him a comprehensive report of all that exists in the land of Canaan.

So they went up and spied out the land from the Wilderness of Zin as far as Rehob, near the entrance of Hamath. And they went up through the South and came to Hebron; Ahiman, Sheshai, and Talmai, the descendants of Anak, were there. (Now Hebron was built seven years before Zoan in Egypt.) Then they came to the Valley of Eshcol, and there cut down a branch with one cluster of grapes; they carried it between two of them on a pole. They also brought some of the pomegranates and figs. The place was called the Valley of Eshcol, because of the cluster which the men of Israel cut down there. And they returned from spying out the land after forty days.[2]

---

1   Numbers 13:17–20
2   Numbers 13:21–25

That is, they spent forty days spying out the whole land. They were able to carry with them some of the fruit of the land as Moses had commanded them, and after that, they retuned.

> Now they departed and came back to Moses and Aaron and all the congregation of the children of Israel in the Wilderness of Paran, at Kadesh; they brought back word to them and to all the congregation, and showed them the fruit of the land.[3]

And now let us listen to the report they presented.

> Then they told him, and said: "We went to the land where you sent us. It truly flows with milk and honey, and this is its fruit. [That is, the grapes, pomegranates, and figs which they brought back]. Nevertheless the people who dwell in the land are strong; the cities are fortified and very large; moreover we saw the descendants of Anak there. The Amalekites dwell in the land of the South; the Hittites, the Jebusites, and the Amorites dwell in the mountains; and the Canaanites dwell by the sea and along the banks of the Jordan."[4]

---

3   Numbers 13:26
4   Numbers 13:27–29

The twelve men were split into two groups: the first consisting of ten men, the second consisting of two men, who were Joshua the son of Nun and Caleb the son of Jephunneh.

> Then Caleb quieted the people before Moses, and said, "Let us go up at once and take possession, for we are well able to overcome it." But the men who had gone up with him said, "We are not able to go up against the people, for they are stronger than we."[5]

Fear took hold of them, and therefore they said: "We are not able to go up, for they are stronger than we," while Caleb said: "We are able to take possession of this land, and by the grace of God we will be victors against the people inhabiting it." But what was the result of what the ten men said?

> And they gave the children of Israel a bad report of the land which they had spied out, saying, "The land through which we have gone as spies is a land that devours its inhabitants, and all the people whom we saw in it are men of great stature. There we saw the giants (the descendants of Anak came from the giants); and we were like

---

5   Numbers 13:30–31

grasshoppers in our own sight, and so we were in their sight."[6]

Fear of the people of the land of Canaan prevailed in the hearts of these ten men, and they began spreading this fear among the people of Israel. Although Joshua and Caleb said that they are able to possess this land, all the people went after the ten men.

Because of this fear, the anger of God was aroused exceedingly, for they had forgotten His power and His help, and how He took them out of the land of Egypt with a strong hand and with an outstretched arm. Therefore, He made them wander in the wilderness for forty years and they all perished, and none of them entered the promised land except Joshua the son Nun and Caleb the son of Jephunneh. As we read in Deuteronomy (1:21–28):

"Look, the LORD your God has set the land before you; go up and possess it, as the LORD God of your fathers has spoken to you; do not fear or be discouraged." And every one of you came near to me and said, "Let us send men before us, and let them search out the land for us, and bring back word to us of the way by which

---

6   Numbers 13:32–33

we should go up, and of the cities into which we shall come."[7]

That is, God said to them to go up to possess the land.

The plan pleased me well; so I took twelve of you men, one man from each tribe. And they departed and went up into the mountains, and came to the Valley of Eshcol, and spied it out. They also took some of the fruit of the land in their hands and brought it down to us; and they brought back word to us, saying, "It is a good land which the LORD our God is giving us." Nevertheless you would not go up ...[8]

Why did they refuse to go up? Because of fear. Fear makes a person rebel against the command of the Lord. The passage continues:

... but rebelled against the command of the LORD your God; and you complained in your tents, and said, "Because the LORD hates us, He has brought us out of the land of Egypt to deliver us into the hand of the Amorites, to destroy us. Where can we go up? Our brethren [i.e. the ten

---

7   Deuteronomy 1:21–22

8   Deuteronomy 1:23–26

men who spied out the land] have discouraged our hearts, saying, 'The people are greater and taller than we; the cities are great and fortified up to heaven; moreover we have seen the sons of the Anakim there.'"[9]

From the aforementioned, it is clear that they did not enter the promised land and they perished in the wilderness because of fear. And this reminds us of a very important verse mentioned in the Book of Revelation which spoke about the heavenly Jerusalem and the promised land for the believers, saying, "But the cowardly, unbelieving, abominable, murderers, sexually immoral, sorcerers, idolaters, and all liars shall have their part in the lake which burns with fire and brimstone, which is the second death."[10] Fear (cowardice) is one of the reasons for not entering the kingdom, as it happened with the children of Israel who feared in the Wilderness of Sinai, and did not enter the promised land.

This does not, however, mean that every human being who fears has sinned and will not enter the kingdom of heaven. Not every kind of fear is what the Book of Revelation is speaking about.

---

9   Deuteronomy 1:26–28

10   Revelation 21:8

1

Kinds of Fear

His Holiness Pope Shenouda III divides fear into three kinds: godly fear, natural fear, and pathological fear.

Godly Fear

Godly fear means the fear of God, as we pray in the Prayer of Thanksgiving: "Grant us to complete this holy day and all the days of our life in all peace in Your fear." The Scripture says: "The fear of the LORD is the beginning of wisdom."[11] The fear of God means the reverence of God; therefore, we often hear the deacon crying out, saying, "Stand in the fear of God"[12] and "Worship God in fear and trembling."[13] The fear of

---

11   Psalm 111:10

12   Introduction to the gospel in the Coptic Lectionary.

13   The Divine Liturgy according to St. Basil – the liturgy of the faithful

God means worshipping God with all reverence and solemnity. It also means obedience to God and doing His commandments; likewise also, the fear of standing before God on the awesome judgement day[14] in which He will recompense each one according to His deeds.[15]

This fear is godly and is required for the edification of the spiritual person. The Book of Acts mentions: "Then the churches throughout all Judea, Galilee, and Samaria had peace and were edified. And walking in the fear of the Lord and in the comfort of the Holy Spirit, they were multiplied."[16]

The person who does not know the fear of God is a sinful person, capable of committing any sin without fear or shame, because the fear of the Lord has disappeared from his heart.

Natural Fear

A person here may have a fear of darkness, or of the unknown, or of a sudden movement. As previously mentioned, [the fear of] death falls under this kind of natural fear, because it is a fear of the unknown.

---

14 See Agpeya – Litanies of Second Watch of Midnight Hour.

15 See Divine Liturgy According to St. Basil – Liturgy of the Faithful.

16 Acts 9:31.

Pathological Fear

This often is called "phobia" or "paranoia." The person, who has a mental illness, imagines (for example) that there are people wanting to hurt him, even though there may be no one who wants to hurt him. It is his mental illness generating in him these illusions and imaginations.

There also is another kind of pathological fear: the fear that is unwarranted or that has no reason, as is the case with children. Therefore, it is called a childish fear. A person, for example, might imagine that there are thieves in the house or "evil spirits." We do not object to this kind of fear, because it requires specialists in psychiatry. We here, however, will speak about fear as a sin of weakness of faith, which is what happened with the ten spies. This fear might become a sin that deprives the person from entering the kingdom of heaven, because this kind of fear is not from God, and persisting in it may paralyze us and prevent us from continuing our journey with God, "for God has not given us a spirit of fear, but of power and of love and of a sound mind."[17]

---

17   2 Timothy 1:7

2

Causes of Fear

1. Lack of Faith and of Trust in God

Our Lord Christ, therefore, reproved His disciples, saying, "Why are you fearful, O you of little faith?"[18] If the person had faith in God, he would not fear nor be troubled. The Holy Scripture says: "The LORD is my light and my salvation; whom shall I fear? The LORD is the strength of my life; of whom shall I be afraid?... Though an army may encamp against me, my heart shall not fear; though war may rise against me, in this I will be confident."[19] Also, "Yea, though I walk through the valley of the shadow of death, I will fear no evil; for You are with me."[20] Therefore, the fear resulting from a lack

18   Matthew 8:26

19   Psalm 27:1, 3

20   Psalm 23:4

of faith is considered sin, for the person does not believe nor trusts in the power of God.

We must recognize that fear entered into the world because of sin, since we read that after Adam and Eve fell into sin, Adam said to the Lord: "I heard Your voice in the garden, and I was afraid because I was naked; and I hid myself."[21]

2. Committing Sin

If a little child, for example, did something wrong at home, he would fear his parents. Likewise, if a person made a mistake at work, they would fear that this mistake would be discovered. The thief has fear while stealing lest he get caught and get arrested; and so, sin and wrong behavior generate fear in the heart of the person.

3. Focusing on the Surrounding Circumstances More Than Focusing on the Lord

This is what happened with the ten spies. Had their eyes been on the Lord, they would not have feared,

---

21   Genesis 3:10

but instead, they looked at the fortified cities and the descendants of Anak, and they looked at themselves and they saw that they were like grasshoppers before them, and so they were in their sight [i.e. the descendants of Anak's sight]. This also happened with Peter when he said to the Lord: "'Lord, if it is You, command me to come to You on the water.' So He said, 'Come.' And when Peter had come down out of the boat, he walked on the water to go to Jesus."[22] Peter continued walking on the water as long as his eyes were focused on the Lord Christ. But as soon as his eyes went down from the Lord Christ and he saw the circumstances surrounding him t: "when he saw that the wind was boisterous, he was afraid; and beginning to sink."[23]

What had made Stephen endure being stoned, despite the fact that death by stoning is one of the most excruciating kinds of death, as the person dies slowly while the stones pile up on him? Despite this, Stephen was not afraid of death and did not fear being stoned, but on the contrary, he prayed for those stoning him, saying, "Lord, do not charge them with this sin."[24] Stephen turned away his eyes from the stones, and gazed into heaven, and thus saw heaven opened: "And

22 Matthew 14:28–29

23 Matthew 14:30

24 Acts 7:60

18

he said, 'Look! I see the heavens opened and the Son of Man standing at the right hand of God!'"[25] This sight gave him comfort and power, "for God has not given us a spirit of fear, but of power and of love and of a sound mind."[26]

4. Putting Limitations on God's Capabilities and Powers

The person may think that there are things God is not able to do, as it happened with Mary and Martha who said to the Lord Christ when He went to raise their brother: "Lord, if You had been here, my brother would not have died."[27] Their view of the Lord Christ was that He has the power to only heal the sick, but who cannot raise from the dead. For this reason, the Lord said to Martha: "Your brother will rise again,"[28] but what did she answer? "Martha said to Him, 'I know that he will rise again in the resurrection at the last day."[29] For she could not comprehend that God is able to raise him from the dead presently; all that she could imagine is that He can

---

25 Acts 7:56

26 2 Timothy 1:7

27 John 11:32

28 John 11:23

29 John 11:24

heal sicknesses only. Therefore, Jesus said to her: "Did I not say to you that if you would believe you would see the glory of God?"[30] The women could not understand until He said to them: "Where have you laid him?"[31] They thought He wanted to go to the tomb to weep, but were surprised by Him saying to them: "Take away the stone."[32] Martha, the sister of him who was dead, said to Him, "Lord, by this time there is a stench, for he has been dead four days."[33] It is as though she is saying to Him: "Lord, You came too late. If You had been here from the beginning, You would have healed him from his sickness." Jesus, however, "cried with a loud voice, 'Lazarus, come forth!' And he who had died came out."[34]

Sometimes we fear because we believe that God is not able to deal with some of the difficult situations we are passing through. If we realize that God can do everything and no purpose of His can be withheld from Him,[35] fear will have no place in our life. For this reason, Moses the prophet said to the people of Israel:

"Then I said to you, 'Do not be terrified, or afraid

---

30 John 11:40
31 John 11:34
32 John 11:39
33 Ibid.
34 John 11:43–44
35 See Job 42:2

of them. The LORD your God, who goes before you, He will fight for you, according to all He did for you in Egypt before your eyes.'"[36]

Yes, the cities are fortified, the men are giants, but our God is stronger, for He is the Lord strong and mighty, who is mighty conquering in war.[37] God's power has no limits, for He is the Omnipotent. It is as Job has said: "I know that You can do everything, and that no purpose of Yours can be withheld from You."[38]

5. Having a Sense of Guilt

When a person commits a sin, his conscience begins to upbraid him, so he feels guilty, and fear clings to him in life as it happened with Joseph's brothers. They conspired to kill him, threw him into a well, then sold him to the Ishmaelites. Joseph remained for a while in the house of Potiphar, then spent a while in prison, until he came out and became a ruler[39] in the land of Egypt. After that, there was a famine. And their father sent Joseph's brothers to Egypt to buy grain from

---

36 Deuteronomy 1:29–30.

37 See Psalm 24:8.

38 Job 42:2.

39 Literally: the second man.

their brother Joseph, without knowing that he was their brother. Joseph began to behave with them in a particular way, and hid his silver cup in the mouth of Benjamin's sack, and wanted to keep Benjamin with him. When he put them in prison, Scripture says: "Then they said to one another, 'We are truly guilty concerning our brother, for we saw the anguish of his soul when he pleaded with us, and we would not hear; therefore this distress has come upon us.'"[40] What was the cause of fear in their hearts? It was a sense of guilt, for they felt that they had committed a mistake, and were then reaping the consequence of what they did, though after many years.

> "I sat on the pinnacle of the world, when I realized in myself that I do not fear anything nor desire anything."
>
> — St. Augustine

---

40   Genesis 42:21

3

The Effect of Fear on the Human Being

What does fear generate in the human being?

(1) Fear generates anxiety and disturbance within the human being, and takes joy and peace away from him. Once the person fears and is disturbed, this disturbance is reflected in his body: His heart beats faster, his throat dries up, he loses his peace and joy, and he may suffer from a headache and have difficulty breathing. Scripture mentioned that the disciples, when they saw the Lord Christ after the resurrection, that "they were terrified and frightened,"[41] for they thought that they were seeing a spirit. They began to lose their peace; therefore, the

---

41   Luke 24:37

first word the Lord Christ said to them is "Peace to you." He gave them peace after anxiety, disturbance and fear had taken hold of them. Undoubtedly, we excuse them, for to them, the Lord Christ had died and was buried. Imagine, if a dead buried person walked in on you and the doors were shut, you definitely would be terrified and troubled. Therefore, the Lord Christ gave them peace twice, in John 20:19 ("Jesus came and stood in the midst, and said to them, 'Peace be with you'") and in John 20:21 ("So Jesus said to them again, 'Peace to you!'"). This is what we ask for at the conclusion of the Watos Theotokias: "As You have given to Your holy apostles, likewise say unto us My peace I give to you."

(2) Fear is contagious and spreads rapidly among people. This is what happened when the ten men returned; they [that is, the people] said: "Where can we go up? Our brethren have discouraged our hearts, saying, 'The people are greater and taller than we; the cities are great and fortified up to heaven; moreover we have seen the sons of the Anakim there.'"[42] When a person fears, this fear can easily be transmitted to others. If there were an epidemic or a disease from which some people were

---

42 Deuteronomy 1:28

troubled, fear may spread to all people, and anxiety and fear can begin taking control over them.

In the field of service, also, those who are served love the confident servant who does not fear, but if the servant begins to fear and get troubled, his fear would have negative effects on his service, and then on those whom he is serving. This is the meaning of the verse: "I will strike the shepherd, and the sheep of the flock will be scattered."[43] When the shepherd suffers from fear, the sheep of the flock get worried. This is why when they came to Nehemiah and asked him to hide in the temple because they wanted to kill him, he said to them: "Should such a man as me flee?"[44] Had Nehemiah feared and hid in the temple, the heart of the people following him would have weakened and they would have given up. He had to hold on to his own power and courage, and thereby he could give power to those around him. This is what happened also when His Holiness Pope Shenouda was staying in the monastery (during his exile). Whoever visited him found in him this power, courage and peace, so they would themselves be filled with comfort, power and peace, because they found

---

43 Matthew 26:31

44 Nehemiah 6:11

in their father and shepherd courage and power, and because fear had not infiltrated his heart.

(3) Fear distorts our view of things. The fear, which took over the people of Israel as a result of the bad report which the ten spies gave, distorted their view of the Lord, so they said: "Because the LORD hates us, He has brought us out of the land of Egypt to deliver us into the hand of the Amorites, to destroy us."[45] Yet, we read in the Book of Exodus: "Then the children of Israel groaned because of the bondage, and they cried out; and their cry came up to God because of the bondage. So God heard their groaning, and God remembered His covenant with Abraham, with Isaac, and with Jacob."[46] Now, however, they say that God hates them, and that He delivered them *from* the land of Egypt with a strong hand and with an outstretched arm to deliver them *into* the hand of the Amorites and to destroy them, because He does not love them.

Fear makes the person not look at things in a sound way, and makes him forget the love of God and His care for him in the past, so that he does not remember His numerous benefits. The children of Israel had forgotten

---

45 Deuteronomy 1:27
46 Exodus 2:23–24

how God split the Red Sea before them, and how He gave them Manna from heaven, and brought forth water for them out of the rock;[47] they forgot everything because of fear. Therefore, in the Psalm it says: "Bless the LORD, O my soul, and forget not all His benefits."[48] Forgetting the benefits of God gives rise to fear, and when the person fears, he forgets the benefits of God all the more, and he enters a vicious cycle. But when he remembers the promises of God and His marvelous works, and places them continually before his eyes, his outward appearance always proclaims: "God, who has helped me all these years, will help me to the end."

(4) Fear may be a cause of some psychosomatic illnesses, for there are many who actually suffered from bodily illnesses because of fear and disturbance.

Fear paralyzes the person, and this paralysis prevents them from performing and fulfilling the will of God in his life. God said to Moses: "Look, the LORD your God has set the land before you; go up and possess it, as the LORD God of your fathers has spoken to you; do not fear or be discouraged."[49] The people, however, refused to perform the order and command of God, and refused

---

47   See Nehemiah 9:11, 15

48   Psalm 103:2

49   Deuteronomy 1:21.

to enter the promised land. The same happens with us today; we hesitate to perform the command of the Lord because of fear. Many have a fear of performing the command "whoever slaps you on your right cheek, turn the other to him also."[50] They fear, thinking that others will take advantage of them and will think of them as weaklings. They forget that God gave this command, and is the One also who gives power to perform it; and that it is impossible that God makes His children weak before others, for the children of God are strong. "I have written to you, young men, because you are strong, and the word of God abides in you, and you have overcome the wicked one."[51] Many also do not give tithes, for fear that their income might not be adequate, and they do not guarantee what the future is hiding for them. But if one is adorned with faith and has trust in God, fear will not sneak into his heart.

> "Fear may be an inadequacy and may be transformed into a mental illness. If we, however, transform it into the fear of God, it becomes pure for the pure, and in this way, fear is transformed into a virtue that protects from falling into sin."
>
> — His Holiness Pope Shenouda III

---

50   Matthew 5:39

51   1 John 2:14

(5) Fear stunts the spiritual growth of the person, and might stunt his faith in the Lord Christ as mentioned in the story of the man born blind. When the father and mother were asked about who healed their son, they said, "We do not know," because they feared the Jews, for the Jews had agreed already that if anyone confessed that He was the Christ, he would be put out of the synagogue.[52] This fear made them ignore the commandment and the work of God, so they said, "He is of age; ask him. He will speak for himself."[53] Therefore, St. John says: "Nevertheless even among the rulers many believed in Him, but because of the Pharisees they did not confess Him, lest they should be put out of the synagogue; for they loved the praise of men more than the praise of God."[54] Likewise it says: "The fear of man brings a snare, [when one person fears another and fears the opinions of others of him, this becomes a snare for him], but whoever trusts in the LORD shall be safe."[55]

When Paul the Apostle was accused regarding his apostleship, speaking about him as not being an apostle because he did not see the Lord Christ like the twelve did. He said to them: "But with me it is a very small

---

52 See John 9:22

53 John 9:21

54 John 12:42–43

55 Proverbs 29:25

thing that I should be judged by you or by a human court."[56] That is, it is a very small that I should be judged by a human being; you are not the ones who will decide whether I an an apostle or not, because my apostleship I received from God, "for not he who commends himself is approved, but whom the Lord commends."[57] The person who fears the opinion of others will be transformed into what we call a "men pleaser;" that is, his top priority is to please those around him. Paul the Apostle, however, said with utmost clarity: "For if I still pleased men, I would not be a bondservant of Christ."[58] The fear of the opinion of others may stunt the spiritual growth of the person.

(6) Fear results in complaining and grumbling. When a person fears, he begins asking questions, "Why does God do this, and why does He abandon His people?" And [the person] begins grumbling, and this is what happened with the people of Israel when they feared the people of Anak; it says about them: "And you complained in your tents, and said, 'Because the LORD hates us, He has brought us out of the land of Egypt to deliver us into the hand of the Amorites, to destroy

56   1 Corinthians 4:3

57   2 Corinthians 10:18

58   Galatians 1:10

us.'"[59] Fear makes a person always complain, and makes the person have doubts about the love of God and His care. For this reason we often find that fear is responsible for the person remaining inactive and not contributing positively in life.

(7) Fear paralyzes the person, making him incapable of advancing forward. Fear makes the person think that they will not be able to fulfill their dreams and wishes, and it makes the person remain silent, and not say the truth. This is what made St. Athanasius, when they said to him that the whole world was against him, respond and say, "And I am against the world," because fear had no place in his heart.

We are also reminded of John the Baptist who stood courageously before Herod and convicted him of his sin. It is true that he lost his life on earth, but he won the heavenly crown. Elijah the Prophet also did not remain silent before Ahab the king and was not afraid. Although he ran away from Jezebel after he killed the prophets of Baal, fear beginning to sneak into his heart, God said to him, "What are you doing here, Elijah?"[60]

---

59 Deuteronomy 1:27

60 1 Kings 19:9

Fear is what bridles the tongues of people, preventing them from expressing themselves freely without embarrassment or fear. It is what makes many remain silent from [saying] the word of truth and defending those suffering wrong. It is what makes a person unsuccessful in his life, taking them away from their hopes and dreams, not realizing the achievements they desire to reach.

People should control their reactions toward fear. Otherwise, they lose a great deal of their humanity related to the expression of their selves and defending the truth and those wronged, if they permit their reactivity to take control over them and to paralyze them. When a person is in a state of fear, they become ready to do anything to save themself. For this reason, they employed tortures to make the believers deny Christ, as they wanted to introduce fear into them by releasing lions on them or by scourging them, or by various other torture mechanisms. But the children of God knew no fear because Christ was alive in their hearts, and they did not fear nor were they afraid of death.

We have previously spoken about the fear resulting from sin and the lack of belief in God, (which is different than godly fear or pathological fear). There is a great difference between healthy fear—meaning caution which makes us step back before falling from the top of a mountain—and the fear which takes control over our life and prevents us from excelling and living with power.

> "Fear not untruth, that it spreads out or triumphs. Untruth must be defeated before the steadfastness of the truth, regardless of how long it takes; and for every Goliath there is a David waiting for him and triumphing over him in the name of the Lord of hosts."
>
> — His Holiness Pope Shenouda III

4

How Do We Face Fear?

We have previously dealt with the effect of fear in our life. This fear deprived the children of Israel from entering the promised land, and it is what deprives people from entering heaven, as we have previously pointed to that which is mentioned in the Book of Revelation (21:8). Therefore, it is necessary that fear be faced and dealt with, rather than running away from it.

Now, I would like to recount the story of David and Goliath (1 Samuel 17). David was a youth. He was not a soldier in the army, but was a shepherd of the sheep and was courageous. Goliath would defy the armies of the people of the living God, and no one of the army of Israel dared to answer him with a word, and when they saw the man, they fled from him and were dreadfully afraid.[61] When the youth arrived—who

---

61   See 1 Samuel 17:24

is described by the Scripture as "ruddy, with bright eyes, and good-looking"[62]—and heard the defiance of this man, he stood and said: "For who is this uncircumcised Philistine, that he should defy the armies of the living God?"[63] And he wanted to fight him. When Eliab his oldest brother heard him, his anger was aroused against him and said to him: "Why did you come down here? And with whom have you left these few sheep in the wilderness? I know your pride and insolence of your heart, for you have come down to see the battle."[64] Even King Saul disparaged him and said to him:

> "You are not able to go against this Philistine to fight with him; for you are a youth, and he a man of war from his youth." But David said to Saul, "Your servant used to keep his father's sheep, and when a lion or a bear came and took a lamb out of the flock, I went out after it and struck it, and delivered the lamb from its mouth; and when it arose against me, I caught it by its beard, and struck and killed it. Your servant has killed both lion and bear; and this uncircumcised Philistine will be like one of them, seeing he has defied the armies of the living God." [65]

---

62 1 Samuel 16:12

63 1 Samuel 17:26

64 1 Samuel 17:28

65 1 Samuel 17:33–36

From where did David derive this power? From his faith in God; therefore he did not run away from Goliath, but said to him: "You come to me with a sword, with a spear, and with a javelin. But I come to you in the name of the LORD of hosts."[66] He derived his power from God, and this divine power took fear out of his heart, and he said to Goliath: "This day the LORD will deliver you into my hand."[67] David possessed a heart of a lion because of his strong relationship with God, and through this strong relationship with God, he could face fear and triumph over it.

(1) Look for the cause of fear in your life. The cause may be a sin, and you fear that it becomes revealed before others. Or, the cause may be a lack of faith in God, or a feeling of guilt, or a lack of trust in God's power. Therefore, you have to sit with yourself and search for the cause of fear in your life, and confess before God that your faith is weak. The Gospel of St. Mark mentions a man in the crowd, whose son had an evil spirit, and he came to the Lord Christ to heal him, but the Lord Christ said to him: "If you can believe, all things are possible to him who believes."[68] The man discovered that he

---

66   1 Samuel 17:45

67   1 Samuel 17:46

68   Mark 9:23

did not have faith. "Immediately the father of the child cried out and said with tears, 'Lord, I believe; help my unbelief!'"[69] Here the man confessed his lack of faith and his weakness.

The person has to do their part fully, to triumph over fear. If a person has a fear of an exam, for example, they have to study well, and this will help them overcome the fear. We have to fulfill what we are required to do, and God will give us peace which surpasses all understanding and will take away from us anxiety, trouble and fear.

(2) Ask for the counsel and guidance of others. For example, if a person has an interview to get a particular job, they can take the counsel of some specialists in that field, asking them about how the person may deal with this interview. So, preparing well will diminish the person's fear.

(3) Be assured that God is the ruler of all (Pantocrator). There are many things in our life which we have no authority over and we cannot control; God, however, has authority over everything. Saul was pursuing David, desiring to kill him, but David believed that his life was

---

69 Mark 9:24

in God's hand. So if God had given the authority to Saul to kill him, he would have killed him. And if He had not given him the authority, he would not have been able to kill him anyway. This faith made David not fear, because he was sure that his life was in God's hand. "And we know that all things work together for good to those who love God."[70] This also is what Paul the Apostle confirmed when he was imprisoned in Rome, for he said: "For I know that this will turn out for my deliverance through your prayer and the supply of the Spirit of Jesus Christ."[71] Does this mean that he would be released from prison? Paul says, No, "so now also Christ will be magnified in my body whether by life or by death."[72] I might come out of prison to continue the service or I might come out of prison by going to heaven, and the one making the decision is God. So if He chooses that I come out of prison to heaven, this is a gain to me; but if He chooses that I come out of prison to continue living, to me to live is Christ. Thus, fear did not sneak into Paul's heart, and he was not afraid of death, for the decision of death is not in the hand of Nero, but in the hand of God. So if God is the Ruler of

---

70   Romans 8:28

71   Philippians 1:19

72   Philippians 1:20

all and has authority over everything, why do we fear and become frightened?

Surrender your life to God. As Scripture says: "Trust in the LORD with all your heart, and lean not on your own understanding."[73] If we rely on God, He will grant us His peace which surpasses all understanding.

(4) Remind yourself of God's benefits and His works in your life. Remember the hardships you went through and how God saved you out of them with a strong hand and with an outstretched arm. Remember that "the goodness of God endures continually."[74] This matter grants us courage and takes away fear from our heart.

(5) Reflect on verses from the Holy Scripture, and write them down and keep them before you. There are very many verses in Holy Scripture talking about fear and encouraging us to overcome it: "Be strong and of good courage, do not fear nor be afraid of them; for the LORD your God, He is the One who goes with you. He will not leave you nor forsake you."[75] Remember this promise every morning before you leave your house, for God is with you; He will not leave you nor forsake you.

---

73 Proverbs 3:5

74 Psalm 52:1

75 Deuteronomy 31:6

"The LORD is my light and my salvation; whom shall I fear? The LORD is the strength of my life; of whom shall I be afraid? When the wicked came against me to eat up my flesh, my enemies and foes, they stumbled and fell. Though an army may encamp against me, my heart shall not fear; though war may rise against me, in this I will be confident."[76] The reason for this tranquility is the presence of God with us. "I called on the LORD in distress; the LORD answered me and set me in a broad place. The LORD is on my side; I will not fear."[77] For who would do us evil if God is with us? "Do not be afraid of sudden terror, nor of trouble from the wicked when it comes; for the LORD will be your confidence, and will keep your foot from being caught."[78]

The Book of Isaiah, starting from Chapter 40, is called the book of consolation. Many are the words of consolation and encouragement which came in the Book of Isaiah:

> "You whom I have taken from the ends of the earth, and called from its farthest regions, and said to you, 'You are My servant, I have chosen you and have not cast you away: Fear not, for I

---

76 Psalm 27:1–3

77 Psalm 118:5–6

78 Proverbs 3:25–26

am with you; be not dismayed[79] [for the person who fears is always looking back] for I am your God. I will strengthen you, yes, I will help you, I will uphold you with My righteous right hand.' Behold, all those who were incensed against you shall be ashamed and disgraced; they shall be as nothing, and those who strive with you shall perish. You shall seek them and not find them—those who contended with you. Those who war against you shall be as nothing, as a nonexistent thing. For I, the LORD your God, will hold your right hand, saying to you, 'Fear not, I will help you.' Fear not, you worm Jacob, you men of Israel! I will help you," says the LORD and your Redeemer, the Holy One of Israel. "Behold, I will make you into a new threshing sledge with sharp teeth; you shall thresh the mountains and beat them small, and make the hills like chaff. You shall winnow them, the wind shall carry them away, and the whirlwind shall scatter them; you shall rejoice in the LORD, and glory in the Holy One of Israel. The poor and needy seek water, but there is none, their tongues fail for thirst. I, the LORD, will hear them; I, the God of Israel, will not forsake them. I will open rivers in desolate heights, and fountains in the midst of the valleys; I will make the wilderness a pool of water, and the

---

79 "Dismayed" appears in the NKJV translation; while in Septuagint, the word is "go astray;" the word used in the Arabic verse may be translated to "look back."

dry land springs of water."[80]

All these are words of consolation, putting the person's heart at peace. Keep before you the promises of God, and if fear sneaks into your heart, bring these verses out and read them, and say to God, "Do not forget the covenant which You have made with our fathers, Abraham, Isaac and Jacob. I am Your child and You have said to me, 'I will strengthen you, yes, I will help you, I will uphold you with My righteous right hand.'"

Fear sneaks into the heart of the person who is idle; the devil begins sowing the seeds of doubt and fear. But the person who is occupied, especially with serving God, fear will not sneak into his heart, but he will receive power unto power.

Fear entered the world because of sin, so we began to have the fear of death and the fear of facing God as it happened with Adam when he transgressed the commandment of God. But by repentance and returning to God, this fear comes to an end in the person's heart. The Lord Christ is the only one capable of saving the person from sin, and of granting him true and acceptable repentance, and of giving them peace which surpasses understanding, and of granting them everlasting life

---

80   Isaiah 41:9–18

according to His true promise: "Most assuredly, I say to you, he who hears My word and believes in Him who sent Me has everlasting life, and shall not come into judgement, but has passed from death to life."[81]

---

81   John 5:24

5

Some Verses Emphasizing No Need to Fear

"And the LORD, He is the One who goes before you. He will be with you, He will not leave you nor forsake you; do not fear nor be dismayed."[82]

"And the LORD said to Joshua, 'Do not fear them, for I have delivered them into your hand; not a man of them shall stand before you.'"[83]

"So he answered, 'Do not fear, for those who are with us are more than those who are with them.'"[84]

---

82 Deuteronomy 31:8
83 Joshua 10:8
84 2 Kings 6:16

"And David said to his son Solomon, 'Be strong and of good courage, and do it; do not fear nor be dismayed, for the LORD God—my God—will be with you. He will not leave you nor forsake you, until you have finished all the work for the service of the house of the LORD.'"[85]

"And you, son of man, do not be afraid of them nor be afraid of their words, though briers and thorns are with you and you dwell among scorpions; do not be afraid of their words or dismayed by their looks, though they are a rebellious house."[86]

"Do not fear, little flock, for it is your Father's good pleasure to give you the kingdom."[87]

"Do not fear any of those things which you are about to suffer. Indeed, the devil is about to throw some of you into prison, that you may be tested, and you will have tribulation ten days. Be faithful until death, and I will give you the crown of life."[88]

And all everlasting glory be to our God. Amen.

---

85 1 Chronicles 28:20

86 Ezekiel 2:6

87 Luke 12:32

88 Revelation 2:10

www.ingramcontent.com/pod-product-compliance
Lightning Source LLC
Chambersburg PA
CBHW050842040426
42339CB00014B/85